AF478154

BURT FRANKLIN: BIBLIOGRAPHY & REFERENCE SERIES 379
Essays in Literature & Criticism 99

FRANK NORRIS

Bibliography

and

Biographical Data

FRANK NORRIS
(Benjamin Franklin Norris)

Bibliography

and

Biographical Data

JOSEPH GAER, Editor

BURT FRANKLIN
NEW YORK

Published by LENOX HILL Pub. & Dist. Co. (Burt Franklin)
235 East 44th St., New York, N.Y. 10017
Originally Published: 1935
Reprinted: 1970
Printed in the U.S.A.

S.B.N.: 8337-12578
Library of Congress Card Catalog No.: 71-131408
Burt Franklin: Bibliography and Reference Series 379
Essays in Literature and Criticism 99

T ABLE OF CONTENTS

Prefatory Note

For a long time a genuine need existed for a comprehensive bibliography of Frank Norris' work, so arranged as to enable one to trace the development of his brief career--a career that permanently placed him among America's most significant literary figures.

In arranging the material for this monograph this need was kept in view. Frank Norris' works, published in book form, are presented chronologically, by date of first publication. Each book is followed by a table of contents, with the dates of the original serial publication. These are followed, again chronologically, by all his other works, including fiction and non-fiction, that were never gathered in book form. Thus each composition is accounted for in its place, without duplication. The Index, at the end of the monograph, enables one to find at a glance any one of Frank Norris' works.

We believe, without any undue pride, that this is the most complete bibliography of Frank Norris' work so far assembled; and, what is more important, by arrangement the most useful.

Joseph Gaer

Errata.   In previous monographs some type errors
             have crept in during the stenciling of the
             material. These errors will, of course,
             be corrected when the entire bibliography
             of California Fiction is assembled for
             completion.

F R A N K   N O R R I S

(1870   -   1902)

Bibliography of Fiction

(Publication in which story or article first appeared
 is shown in parentheses.)

MORAN OF THE LADY LETTY

- Novel of Adventure off the Coast of California -

Published by Doubleday & McClure Company, September, 1898.
Republished in Vol. III of "Collected Works of Frank Norris"
issued by Doubleday, Doran & Company, 1928. Introductions
by Kathleen Norris and Rupert Hughes.
London publisher: Grant Richards, 1899. Under title:
   "Shanghaied".

(The Wave, January 8 --
April 9, 1898)

McTEAGUE

- Novel of San Francisco -

Published by Doubleday & McClure Company, February, 1899.
Popular priced edition, by Grossett & Dunlap, 1920, with
illustrations from photoplay, "Greed", adapted from the
novel.
Republished in Vol. VII of "Collected Works of Frank Norris"
issued by Doubleday, Doran & Company, 1928. Introduction
by Theodore Dreiser.
London publishers: Grant Richards, 1899; William Heinemann,
1922.

BLIX

- Semi-biographical Novel -

Published by Doubleday & McClure Company, September, 1889.
Popular priced edition, by Grossett & Dunlap, 1925.
Republished in Vol. III of "Collected Works of Frank
    Norris" issued by Doubleday, Doran & Company, 1928.
    Introductions by Kathleen Norris and Rupert Hughes.
London publisher: Grant Roberts, 1900.

(The Puritan, March-August, 1899)

A MAN'S WOMAN

- Novel of the North -

Published by Doubleday & McClure Company, February, 1900.
Popular priced edition, by the Garden City Publishing
    Company, 1923.
Republished in Vol. VI of "Collected Works of Frank
    Norris" issued by Doubleday, Doran & Company, 1928.
    Introduction by Christopher Morley.
London publisher: Grant Richards, 1900.

(New York Evening Sun &
San Francisco Chronicle,
July-October, 1899)

THE OCTOPUS *

- Novel of the Wheat Fields of California -

Published by Doubleday, Page & Company, April, 1901.
Popular priced edition, by the Garden City Publishing
    Company, 1903.
Republished in Vols. I and II of "Collected Works of
    Frank Norris" issued by Doubleday, Doran & Company,
    1928. Foreword by Irvin S. Cobb.
London publishers: Grant Richards, 1901, under title:
    "The Epic of the Wheat: The Octopus"; J. Nelson &
    Son, 1902.

    * First of a trilogy on human struggle and sacrifice
      which was to include: "The Octopus," where the grain
      was grown; "The Pit," where the product was marketed,
      and "The Wolf," where the wheat was eaten. Norris'
      death prevented the completion of "The Wolf."
      Last book published before Norris' death, October 25,
      1902.

<u>Posthumous Publications</u>

<u>THE PIT</u> *

- Novel of the Chicago Grain Market -

Published by Doubleday, Page & Company, January, 1903.
Popular priced edition, by the Garden City Publishing
  Company, 1903.
Republished in Vol. IX of "Collected Works of Frank
  Norris", issued by Doubleday, Doran & Company, 1928.
  Introduction by Juliet Wilbor Tompkins.
"Modern Library Inc." 1934.
London publishers: Grant Richards, 1903. Under title:
  "The Epic of the Wheat: The Pit". Republished by
  T. Nelson & Son, Ltd., 1932.

(Saturday Evening Post
September 27, 1902 - January 31,1903)

*Adapted into a stage play.

<u>A DEAL IN WHEAT</u>

- Collected Stories -

Published by Doubleday, Page & Company, October, 1903.
Republished in Vol. IV of "Collected Works of Frank
  Norris", issued by Doubleday, Doran & Company, 1928.
  Introduction by Will Irwin.
London publisher: Grant Richards, 1903.

A Deal in Wheat	(Everybody's Magazine, August, 1902; reprinted in Today, English publication, April 22, 1903)
The Wife of Chino	(Century Magazine, Jan. 1903)
A Bargain with Peg-Leg	(Collier's Weekly, March 1, 1902)
The Passing of Cock-Eye Blacklock	(Century Magazine, July 1902; reprinted in California Story Book, University of California, 1909)
A Memorandum of Sudden Death	(Collier's Weekly, January 11, 1902)
Two Hearts that Beat as One	(Brander Magazine)
Dual Personality of Slick Dick Nickerson	(Collier's Weekly, November 22, 1902)
The Ship that Saw a Ghost	(Overland Monthly, December, 1902)
The Ghost in the Cross-Trees	(New York Herald, March, 1903)
The Riding of Felipe	(Everybody's Magazine, March, 1901)

<u>FRANK NORRIS: COMPLETE WORKS</u>*

- First Uniform Edition -

Issued by Doubleday, Page & Company, 1903.

Vol.   I - "Blix" and "Moran of the Lady Letty".
Vol.   II - "A Deal in Wheat".
Vol.   III - "McTeague".
Vol.   IV - "A Man's Woman".
Vol.   V - "The Octopus".
Vol.   VI - "The Pit".
Vol.   VII - "Responsibilities of a Novelist".

*Limited to 100 sets.

<u>THE JOYOUS MIRACLE</u>

- Short Story -

Published by Doubleday, Page & Company, October, 1906.
Republished in Vol. VII of "Collected Works of
   Frank Norris" issued by Doubleday, Doran & Company
   1928.   Foreword by Grant Overton; introduction by
   C. C. Dobie.
London publishers: Harper & Brothers, 1906.

                     (The Wave, October 9, 1897, under
                      title: "Miracle Joyeux" reprinted
                      in McClure's Magazine, December
                      1898)

<u>THE THIRD CIRCLE</u>

- Collected Stories -

Published by John Lane, June, 1909.
Republished in Vol. IV of "Collected Works of Frank
   Norris" issued by Doubleday, Doran & Company, 1928.
   Introduction by Will Irwin.
London publisher: John Lane, 1909.

The **Third** Circle   (The Wave, August 28, 1897; re-
                                   printed in the Golden Book,
                                   January, 1931)
The House with the Blinds (The Wave, August 21, 1897)
Little Dramas of the   (The Wave, January 26 and
   Curbstone (Sketches,   December 10, 1897)
   signed "Justin Sturgis")

<u>The Third Circle continued</u>:

Shorty Stack, Pugilist	(The Wave, November 20, 1897)
The Strangest Thing	(" " July 3, 1897)
A Reversion to Type	(" " August 14, 1897)
Boom	(" " August 7, 1897)
The Dis-Associated Charities	(" " October 30, 1897, under title: "The Associated Un-Charities".
The Son of the Sheik	(The Argonaut, June 1, 1891. Unsigned)
A Defense of the Flag	(" Argonaut, October 28, 1895)
Toppan	(Berklyian Magazine, September 22, 1893; reprinted in Christmas Number of The Wave, 1893, under title: "Unequally Yoked".)
A Caged Lion	(The Argonaut, August 20, 1894; reprinted in the Argonaut, November 7, 1902)
This Animal of a Buldy Jones	(The Wave, July 17, 1897; reprinted in McClure's Magazine, March 1899)
Dying Fires	(Smart Set Magazine, July, 1902)
Grettier at Drangey	(Everybody's Magazine, March, 1902)
The Guest of Honor	(Pilgrim Magazine, July and August, 1902)

<u>VANDOVER AND THE BRUTE</u> *

- Novel -

(with a San Francisco Background)

Published by Doubleday, Page & Company, April, 1914.
Republished in Vol. V of "Collected Works of Frank
    Norris" issued by Doubleday, Doran & Company, 1928.
    Introduction by H. L. Mencken.
London publisher: William Heinemann, 1914.

*Begun while a student at Harvard, the manuscript
    was found twelve years after Frank Norris' death
    by his brother, Charles G. Norris, in a trunk that
    had passed through the San Francisco fire.

COLLECTED WORKS OF FRANK NORRIS

- Second Uniform Edition -

Issued by Doubleday, Doran & Company, 1928.

```
Vol.   I - "The Octopus".
Vol.  II -  "     "      (Continued)
Vol. III - "Blix" and "Moran of the Lady Letty".
Vol.  IV - "The Third Circle" and "A Deal in Wheat".
Vol.   V - "Vandover and the Brute".
Vol.  VI - "A Man's Woman" and "Yvernelle".
Vol. VII - "Responsibilities of the Novelist, and
                  "The Joyous Miracle".
Vol.VIII - "McTeague".
Vol.  IX - "The Pit".
Vol.   X - Collected Writings (See Below)
```

COLLECTED WRITINGS

- Hitherto Unprinted in Book Form -

Being Vol. X of "Collected Writings of Frank Norris".
(See above)   Introduction by Charles G. Norris.

Stories from the San Francisco Wave:

```
Le Jongleur of Taillebois       (December 25, 1891)
A Salvation Boom in Matabeland  (April 25, 1896)
The Heroism of Jonesee          (May 16, 1896)
A Case for Lombroso             (September 11, 1897)
His Single Blessedness          (September 18, 1897)
His Dead Mother's Portrait      (November 13, 1897)
Man Proposes:
     Number 1 -                 (May 23, 1896)
        "    2 -                 (May 30, 1896)
        "    3 -                 (June 13, 1896)
        "    4 -                 (June 27, 1896)
        "    5 -                 (July 4, 1896)
```

Articles and Sketches from the San Francisco Wave:
Suggestions: I - 1870. II - A Hotel Room, III -
Brute. (March, 1897) The End of the Act (Originally
published in the Harvard Crimson; reprinted in The
Wave, November 27, 1897)

```
A South Sea Expedition          (February 20, 1897)
New Years at San Quentin        (January 9, 1897)
A Lag's Release                 (March 27, 1897)
Among Cliff Dwellers            (May 15, 1897)
Sailing of the Excelsior        (July 31, 1897)
Passing of Little Pete          (January 30, 1897)
```

(continued)

<u>Collected Writings continued</u>:

Stories from the Overland Monthly:
    Lauth   (March, 1893)
    Travis Hallett's Half-Back   (January, 1894)
    Outward and Visible Signs:
      I - She and the Other Fellow (March, 1894)
     II - The Most Notable
            Conquest of Man   (May, 1894)
    III - Outside of Zenana   (July 1894)
     IV - After Strange Gods   (October, 1894)
      V - Thoroughbred   (February, 1895)

South African Articles:
    A Californian in the City of   (San Francisco Chronicle,
        Cape Town   January 19, 1896)
    From Cape Town to Kimberley   (San Francisco Chronicle,
        Mines   January 26, 1896)
    In the Compound of a Diamond (San Francisco Chronicle,
        Mine   February 2, 1896)
    In the Veldt of the Transvaal (San Francisco Chronicle,
                            February 9, 1896)
    A Zulu War Dance   (San Francisco Chronicle,
                            March 15, 1896)

    Jack Hammond in Johannesburg
        and Pretoria   (The Wave, June 20, 1896)

Spanish War Articles:
    With Lawson at El Caney   (Century Magazine,
                           June, 1899)
    Santiago's Surrender   (Syndicated: later
                           printed in pamphlet
                           form by Paul Elder & Co.)
    Comida: An Experience in   (Atlantic Monthly,
        Famine   March, 1899)

Later Short Stories:
    A Statue in an Old Garden   (Ladies Home Journal,
                            May, 1903)
    A Lost Story   (Century Magazine,
                           July, 1903)
    Buldy Jones, Chef du Claque (Everybody's Magazine,
        (Sequel to "This Animal of May, 1901
        a Buldy Jones")

FRANK NORRIS OF THE WAVE

- Collected Stories, Sketches and Articles from the
  Files of the San Francisco Wave - Illustrated.
  Foreword by Charles G. Norris; introduction by
  Oscar Lewis.

Published by the Westgate Press, February, 1931. Printed
by the Grabhorn Press, edition limited to 500 copies.
London publishers: Marshall Simpkins, Ltd., 1931.

Bandy Callaghan's Girl	(April 18, 1896)
His Sister	(November 28, 1896)
The End of the Beginning	(September 4, 1897)
Judy's Service of Gold Plate	(October 16, 1897)
Fantaisie Printaniere	(November 6, 1897)
Perverted Tales: Parodies on the writings of Rudyard Kipling, Stephen Crane, Bret Harte, Richard Harding Davis, Ambrose Bierce and Anthony Hope	(December 24, 1897)

Articles:

The Santa Cruz Venetian Carnival	(July 27, 1896)
A California Jubilee	(July 11, 1896)
Hunting Human Game	(January 23, 1897)
The Bombardment	(April 3, 1897)
At Home from Eight to Twelve	(January 1, 1898)
Cosmopolitan San Francisco	(December 18, 1897)
Reviews and Interviews	
I - Fiction in Review	(July 18, 1896)
II - Mallard's Tales	(August 21, 1897)
III - Lackaye "Making-up"	(December 5, 1896)
IV - Mrs. Carter at Home	(August 14, 1897)
V - Belasco on Plays	(August 28, 1897)
VI - A California Artist	(February 6, 1897)

Dialogues:

In the Heat of Battle	(December 19, 1896)
The Puppets and the Puppy	(May 22, 1897)
Through a Glass Darkly	(June 12, 1897)
The Isabella Regina	(November 27, 1897)

<u>Dialogues - continued</u>:

        Opinions of Leander (Signed "Justin Sturgis"):
            I - Holdeth Forth Upon
                Our Boys and the Ways
                of Them   (July 24, 1897)
           II - Commenteth At Length
                upon Letters Received   (July 31, 1897)
          III - Falleth from Grace and
                Subsequently from a
                Springboard   (August 7, 1897)
           IV - Showing the Plausible
                Mistakes of a Misguided
                Eastern Man   (August 14, 1897)
            V - Opinions of Justin
                Sturgis by Leander   (August 21, 1897)

Sketches:

    A Miner Interviewed   (July 24, 1897)
    When a Woman Hesitates (Signed
        "Justin Sturgis")   (May 29, 1897)
    Western City Types:
            I - The Plumber's
                Apprentice   (May 2, 1896)
           II - The Fast Girl   (May 9, 1896)
          III - An Art Student   (May 16, 1896)

<u>Non-Fiction Books</u>   ---

<u>RESPONSIBILITIES OF THE NOVELIST</u>

- Collected Essays -

Published by Doubleday, Page & Company, October, 1903.
Republished in Vol. VII of "Collected Works of Frank Norris"
    issued by Doubleday, Doran & Company, 1928. Foreword by
    Grant Overton; introduction by Charles Caldwell Dobie.
London publisher: Grant Richards, 1903.

The Responsibilities of the (The Critic, December, 1902)
    Novelist
The True Reward of the   (World's Work, October, 1901)
    Novelist
The Novel with a Purpose   ("   "   May, 1902)
Story Tellers vs. Novelists ("   "   March, 1902)
The Need of a Literary   ("   "   May, 1902)
    Conscience
A Neglected Epic   ("   "   December, 1902)
The Frontier Gone at Last   ("   "   February, 1902)
The Great American Novelist (Syndicated, January 19, 1903)
New York as a Literary
    Centre

<u>Responsibilities of the Novelist con't.</u>

The American Public and "Popular Fiction"	(Syndicated, February 2, 1903)
Child Stories for Adults	(" February 9, 1903)
Newspaper Criticism and American Fiction	(" March 9, 1903)
Novelists to Order - While You Wait	(" February 23, 1903)
The "Nature" Revival in Literature	(" February 16, 1903)
The Mechanics of Fiction	(" December 4, 1901)
Fiction Writing as a Business	(" January 1, 1902)
The Volunteer Manuscript	(" December 11, 1901; reprinted in the Author's Year Book, 1902)

Retail Bookseller: Literary Dictator	(Syndicated, November 20, 1901)
An American School of Fiction	(" January 22, 1902)
Novelists of the Future	(" November 27, 1901)
A Plea for Romantic Fiction	(" December 18, 1901)
A Problem in Fiction	(" November 6, 1901)
Why Women Should Write the Best Novels	(
Symplicity in Art	(" January 15, 1902)

Salt and Sincerity: Series
  of Seven articles Comment-
  ing on Literature's Trend.
  Appearing in "The Critic"
  April to October, 1902.
  Four Selected for this
  Volume.
	(The Critic, May, July, August
	and September, 1902)

    * Contains bibliography up to October, 1903

THE SURRENDER OF SANTIAGO

- Syndicated Cuban War Correspondence -

Published in pamphlet form by Paul Elder & Company, May, 1917.
Republished in Vol. X of "Collected Works of Frank Norris"
  issued by Doubleday, Doran & Company, 1928, under title:
  "Santiago's Surrender".

<u>Poems and a Play</u>:

YVERNELLE *

- Poem -

Published by J. B. Lippencott & Company, October, 1891.
Republished in Vol. VI of "Collected Works of Frank Norris"
   issued by Doubleday, Doran & Company, 1928.

    * This was Frank Norris' first book, printed when
     he was 21.

CREPUSCULM

- Poem -

Published in "Frank Norris, 1870-1902", a pamphlet written
   by Charles G. Norris, 1914.

            (Overland Monthly, April, 1892. re-
              printed in "The Story of the Files",
             Overland Monthly, April, 1892)

<u>FRANK NORRIS</u>: TWO POEMS AND KIM REVIEWED

Edited by Harvey Taylor.
Printed by the Calmar Press, 1930, (Edition limited to 200
   copies.)

Contents:

BRUNHILDE   (poem) signed "Norrys '94"
                Originally published in <u>The Occident</u>
                November 21, 1890. Reprinted in <u>The</u>
                <u>California Illustrated Magazine</u>, with
                illustrations by the Author, June 1892

CREPUSCULM
                Published in "Frank Norris, 1870-1902",
                a pamphlet written by Charles G.
                Norris, 1914.

                    (Overland Monthly, April 1892.
                    Reprinted in "The Story of the
                    Files" in Overland Monthly,
                    April 1892)

"MR. KIPLING'S 'KIM"
                First published (unsigned) in
                <u>World's Work</u>, October, 1901.

<u>Frank Norris: Two Poems and Kim Reviewed - Con't</u>:

BIBLIOGRAPHY of Frank Norris' Work.

PORTRAIT of Frank Norris by Clairice Collins.

<u>TWO PAIR</u> *

- Farce -

Produced by the Junior Class, University of California,
   December 10, 1892.
Published in "California Plays and Pageants" issued by
   the English Club of the University, 1913.

> (Blue and Gold '94, college
> annual, with illustrations by
> the author)

*Manuscript in University of California
   Library.

<u>ARTICLES</u>, <u>ESSAYS</u>, <u>INTERVIEWS</u>, <u>POEMS</u>, <u>REVIEWS</u>, <u>SKETCHES</u>
<u>STORIES</u>

(Not Appearing in Book Form -- Arranged Chronologically)

<u>1889</u>

"Clothes of Steel" Armor   (Unsigned Article)(San Francisco
   of the Middle Ages   Chronicle, October 31)

<u>1890</u>

At Damietta, A. D. 1250
   (Poem - signed "Norrys '94") (The Occident, October 31)

<u>1891</u>

"Stepterfetchit" (Parodies,
   signed: "Norrys '94")
      Dick Wincey   (The Occident, March 27)
      Carl Aisle   ("   "   April 3)
      "Mick" Auley   ("   "   April 10)
"The Finding of Lieutenant
   Outhwaite" (Story)   ("   "   March 13)

<u>Articles, Essays, etc., continued</u>:

Contributions to University of   ("Smiles", October 15,
  California humorous journal   October 30, November 18,
  while associate editor   December 7, December 18)
"The Great Szarratar Opal"
  (Sketch)   ("Smiles", November 18)
"Babazzouin" (Story)   (The Argonaut, May)
"Pottier" (Medevial Ballad) (Berklyian Magazine)

<u>1892</u>

"Archne" (Story)   (The Wave)
"The Way of the World (Story) (" " July 26)

<u>1893</u>

"The Class of '94" (Signed: (Blue and Gold '93,
  "Class Historian)   University of California
                     Annual)

<u>1894</u>

"The Class of '94" (Signed:
  "Class Historian")   (Blue and Gold '94)

<u>1895</u>

"The End of the Act" (Sketch) (Harvard Advocate, April 3.
                    Appears as opening of Chapter
                    14, "Vandover and the Brute")
"A California Vintage (Article) (The Wave, October 12)

<u>1896</u>

"The Uprising in the   (San Francisco Chronicle,
  Transvaal" (Article)   February 9)
"The Frantic Rush from   (San Francisco Chronicle,
  Johannesburg" (Article) March 1)
"Street Scene in Johannesburg (Harper's Weekly, March 1)
  During the Insurrection of
  January, 1896" (Article)
"Rhodes and the Reporters" (The Wave, May 2)
      (Article)
"Types of Western Men: The
  College Man" (Sketch-signed:
  "Marmaduke Masters")   (The Wave, April 25)
"Theory and Reality" (Review) (" " May 2)
"The Benefit Field Day for the (" " May 9)
  California-Eastern Team"
  (Unsigned Article)
"Man Hunting" (Unsigned Article)(" " June 12)
"The Stage and California Girls"
  (Interview)   (" " June 30)

- 16 -

<u>Articles, Essays, etc., cont't: 1896</u>

"Zola as a Romantic Writer"
   (Unsigned Editorial)   (The Wave, June 27)
Stephen Crane's Stories of Life
   in the Slums" (Unsigned Review) ("   "   July 4)
"A Summer in Arcady" (Unsigned
   Review)   ("   "   July 11)
"The Bivalve at Home" (Article)   ("   "   October 3)
"Trilby and Princess Flavia"
   (Review)   ("   "   October 10)
"On a Battleship (Article)   ("   "   October 17)
"Maud Odell and Zenda"   ("   "   October 17)
   (Interview)
"The Evolution of a Nurse"
   (Article)   ("   "   October 17)
"The Week's Football" (Article) ("   "   October 17)
"Italy in California"   "   ("   "   October 24)
"Recreating a University" "   ("   "   October 31)
"Moving a Fifty-Ton Gun   "   ("   "   November 7)
"Election Night on a Daily (Article("   "   November 7)
"The Making of a Pianiste"
   (Interview)   ("   "   November 14)
"A Day with the University of
   California Team" (Article)   ("   "   November 14)
"The Stanford Eleven at Home"
   (Article)   ("   "   November 21)
"The English Courses in the
   University of California"
   (Unsigned Editorial)   ("   "   November 28)
"The Sketch Club Exhibit" (Article)("   "   November 28)
"How it Strikes the Observer:
   The Horse Show" (Article)   ("   "   December 12)
"College Athletics" (Article)   ("   "   December 12)
"Waiting for Their Cue" (Article) ("   "   December 12)
"A Question of Ideals"   "   ("   "   December 26)

1897

"A College Man as a Feature of
   San Francisco Society"
   (Unsigned Editorial)   (The Wave, January 2)
"Inside an Organ" (Article)   ("   "   January 2)
"Where Tamales are Made" (Article) ("   "   January 16)
"Fifi" (Translation from the
   French of Leon Faran)   ("   "   January 23)
"The Decline of the Magazine
   Short Story" (Unsigned Edi-
   torial)   ("   "   January 23)
"One Kind of a New Woman" (Article)("   "   January 30)
"The University of California
   Track Team" (Article)   ("   "   February 6)

<u>1897 continued:</u>

"The Making of a Statue" (Article)	(The Wave, February 13)
"A South Sea Expedition" "	(" " February 20)
"Suggestions: "1870" "A Hotel Room", "Brute", "The Dental Parlors" (sketches)	(" " March 13)
"A Lag's Release" (Article)	(" " March 27)
"The Scoop" (Sketch - signed "Justin Sturgis")	(" " March 27)
"The Bombardment" (Sketch - signed "Justin Sturgis")	(" " April 3)
"A Bitter Bit" (Interview - signed "Justin Sturgis")	(" " April 17)
"Pictures to Burn" (Article - signed "Justin Sturgis")	(" " May 1)
"An Opening for a Novelist (Article)	(" " May 22)
"Metropolitan Noises" (Unsigned ")	(" " May 22)
"Beer and Skittles" (Story)	(" " May 22)
"Fawley's New Beauty" (Interview)	(" " May 29)
"Thief for Twenty Minutes A" (Story signed "Justin Sturgis")	(" " June 5)
"Pseudo-Architecture" (Article signed: "Justin Sturgis")	(" " June 12)
"A Strange Relief Ship" (Unsigned Article)	(" " June 12)
"Training of a Fireman" (Article)	(" " June 12)
"Not Guilty" (Translation from the French of Marcal L'Heureauz, signed "Justin Sturgis")	(" " June 19)
"The Question" (Unsigned Review)	(" " June 19)
"The Marriage Problem" (Article, signed: "Justin Sturgis")	(" " June 26)
"Imitators of Noah" (Unsigned article)	(" " June 26)
"The Cruiser Hi-Yei" (Article)	(" " July 3)
"Miss Sabel's Husband" (Interview)	(" " July 3)
"The Bicycle Gymkhana" (Article, signed "Justin Sturgis")	(" " July 10)
"The Opinions of Leander" (Dialogue, signed "Justin Sturgis". Five of the later dialogues of the series appear in "Frank Norris of the Wave.)	(" " July 17)
"The Upper Office at Work (Article)	(" " July 31)
"New Books" (Review)	(" " July 31)
"A Cat and Dog Life" (Interview)	(" " August 7)
"From Field to Storehouse" (Unsigned Article)	(" " August 7)
"Evolution of a Freshman" (Unsigned Article)	(" " August 21)

<u>1897 continued:</u>

"The Story of a Wall" (Translated
    from the French of Pierre Loti)   (The Wave, August 28)
"Ethics of the Freshman Rush"
    (Unsigned Editorial)   ("   "   September 4)
"Fiction is Selection" (Editorial
    signed: "Justin Sturgis")   ("   "   September 11)
"Dago Conspirators" (Article, signed
    "Justin Sturgis")   ("   "   September 18)
"Crane in London" (Article signed:
    "Justin Sturgis")   ("   "   September 18)
"The Tale and the Truth" (Article)   ("   "   September 25)
"Art Education in San Francisco"
    (Article, signed: "Justin
    Sturgis")   ("   "   September 25)
"The Execution Without Judgement"
    (Story)   ("   "   October 2)"
"Art Association Exhibit" (Article
    signed: "Justin Sturgis")   ("   "   November 27)
"The Mira Monte Club" (Article)   ("   "   December 4)
"Happiness by Conquest" (Editorial)   ("   "   December 11)
"Holiday Literature" (Unsigned
    Review)   ("   "   December 11)
"The Postal Telegraph" (Unsigned
    Article)   ("   "   December 18)
"The Drowned Who do Not Die" (Story)   ("   "   December 25)
"Monsieur Le Roy Explains"
    (Interview, signed: "Justin
    Sturgis")   ("   "   December 25)
"Reviews in Brief"   ("   "   December 25)
"An Elopement" (Translated from the
    French of Ferdinand Bloch)   ("   "   December 25)

<u>1898</u>

"Virtue and Actresses" (Article
    signed: "Justin Sturgis")   ("   "   January 8)
"American Diplomats" (Article,
    signed: "Justin Sturgis")   ("   "   January 15)

<u>1900</u>

"Student Life in Paris" (Article)   (Collier's Weekly, May 12)

<u>1901</u>

"The Unknown A thor and the
    Publisher" (Article, signed:
    "A Publisher's Reader")   (World's Work, April)
"Literature in the East (Article)   (Chicago American Art and
                                        Literary Review, May 25)
"Kirkland at Quarter" (Story)   (Saturday Evening Post
                                        December 12)

1902

"Literature of the West: A
  Reply to William R. Lighton"
  (Article)   (Boston Transcript, Jan. 8)
"The National Spirit as Related
  to the Great American Novel"
  (Article)   ("   "   Feb. 5)
"Salt and Sincerity" (Unsigned
  Aphorisms and Articles. Four
  of the series reprinted in
  "The Responsibilities of a   (The Critic, April, June,
  Novelist")   October)
"In Defense of Doctor Lawler"
  (Article)   (The Argonaut, August 11)
"Life in the Mining Region"
  (Article)   (Everybody's Magazine, Sept.)

1903

"Richard Harding Davis"
  (Article)   (Syndicated, January 26)
"Chances of Unknown Writers"
  (Article)   ("   March 2)
"Grettir at Thornhall-Stead"   (Everybody's Magazine
  (Story)   April)

1907

"The Exile's Toast" (Poem)   (The Reader, May)

<u>BIOGRAPHICAL DATA</u>

<u>F R A N K   N O R R I S</u>
(Benjamin Franklin Norris)

<u>(1870</u> - - - - - <u>1902)</u>

Frank Norris was born March 5th, 1870, in Chicago, and christened Benjamin Franklin Norris, Jr. He was one of five children born to Benjamin Franklin Norris and Gertrude (Doggett) Norris. Only two of the children survived childhood: Frank and his younger brother Charles, who also became a well-known writer.

Frank Norris' father, of British ancestry and born on a Michigan farm, apprenticed himself to a jeweler at the age of fourteen. Ultimately he founded his own business in Chicago and prospered in the prosperity following the Civil War. Frank Norris' mother, of New England-Virginia stock, had been a school teacher before her marriage and aspired to a career as an actress. The mother, by education and temperament, was destined to have a strong influence upon her children in the development of their literary tastes.

In 1878 Frank Norris was taken by his parents to Europe for a year. Upon their return he was sent to a private school in Chicago. But more important than his education at school was the education he received from his mother at home through her readings from the works of Scott, Dickens, Browning and Meredith -- readings that continued through Frank Norris' boyhood and greatly conditioned his leanings toward romantic fiction.

1884-1887

In 1884 the Norrises moved to California. They came
to Oakland, and a year later moved to San Francisco.

Frank Norris was sent to a private academy in Belmont,
and later to High School in San Francisco. In 1886 he was
taken out of school because of a fractured arm and also because the boy developed a great interest in art. He was
enrolled in the San Francisco Art Association's classes.

1887-1889

Frank Norris' ambition to study art abroad was realized
in 1887 when his family took him first to England and then to
France. In Paris he became a student at the Atalier Julien.
The parents returned to California but left their son to
continue his art studies in France.

During that period of his art studies Frank Norris
developed an interest in early French literature (particularly Froissart's Chronicles), and in medieval armor. His
interest in medieval life led to his writing "novels" which
he sent serially in letters to his brother, Charles. When
his father learned of his son's interest in writing, he re-
called him from Paris. Still in love with the spirit of
feudalism after his return to San Francisco, Frank Norris
wrote a long narrative poem, Yvernelle: a Legend of Feudal
France, which was published three years later.

<u>1889-1895</u>

After some private tutoring, Frank Norris entered the University of California at Berkeley.   There he began to read Kipling, Richard Harding Davis, and later, Zola. Zola became an important factor in shaping Norris' approach to writing.   During his college years he contributed sketches, poems and short stories to a number of campus publications as well as <u>The Wave</u>, the <u>Argonaut</u> and the <u>Overland Monthly</u>, San Francisco publications.   During those college years, too, he began to gather material for <u>McTeague</u> and <u>Vandover and the Brute</u>.

Dissatisfaction with the English courses and his inability to master the required mathematics, led him to leave the University in 1894 without graduating.

In the same year his father and mother were divorced. This event had a marked influence on Frank Norris' life. It sobered him considerably of his early dilletante poses, and, confronted with the need of shaping his own career at his own expense, his social viewpoint was greatly altered. He went to Harvard for a year to study under Professor Lewis E. Gates who recognized Norris' promising talent and gave him much encouragement. During his year in Harvard, Norris

applied himself diligently to writing _McTeague_; he also
completed _Vandover and the Brute_, which remained in manuscript form until it was discovered and published posthumously in 1914.

1895-1898

In 1895 Frank Norris went to South Africa as a
correspondent for the _San Francisco Chronicle_. He became
involved in Leander Jameson's raid on Johannesburg and was
captured by the Boers. He was ordered to leave the country,
but an attack of African fever kept him there several months.

Upon his return to San Francisco he joined the staff
of _The Wave_, a literary weekly to which he contributed
during his days at the University of California and which
proved invaluable to Norris as an experimental workshop for
his writing. How much work he did for the _Wave_ can be
gathered from the bibliography of his serially published
work.

1898-1900

McClure's Magazine offered Norris an editorial position,
and he went to New York early in 1898. In New York he met
William Dean Howells who read the manuscript of _McTeague_ with
enthusiasm and urged Norris to publish it.
McClure's sent Norris to report the Spanish-American War for
them and for the _New York Sun_. Another attack of the African

fever, at the end of the war, invalidated him and he returned to San Francisco.

In 1899 <u>McTeague</u> was published, and was very favorably received. At this time Norris conceived the idea of writing a trilogy dealing with the production, distribution and consumption of wheat: "The Epic of Wheat". He started on <u>The Octopus</u>, the first part of the trilogy. This first volume had its background in California.

<u>1900-1902</u>

In January, 1900, Norris married Jeanette Black of San Francisco. During this year he applied himself to <u>The Octopus</u>. It's publication, the following year, established Frank Norris as a leading American novelist.

After the publication of <u>The Octopus</u> the Norrises moved to Chicago where he gathered material for the second volume in the trilogy, <u>The Pit</u>, placed in Chicago, world wheat market. At this time he wrote a number of short stories, posthumously collected in <u>A Deal in Wheat</u>, and a number of essays collected in <u>The Responsibilities of the Novelist</u>.

A daughter, Jeanette, was born to the Norrises in February, 1902. Norris finished <u>The Pit</u> in June. It appeared serially in the <u>Saturday Evening Post</u>, but was not published in book form until 1903.

With the completion of <u>The Pit</u>, Frank Norris started out with his family for a trip around the world to gather

material for <u>The Wolf</u>, the third volume in his trilogy on
the Epic of Wheat.   They went no further than San Francisco.

His trip and his great promise as a writer were
terminated on October 25th, 1902, when Frank Norris, at the
age of thirty-two, died of peritonitis three days after an
appendectomy.

He was buried in the Mountain View Cemetery at Oakland.

N O T E

Though Frank Norris' creative work was in-
terrupted by death very early in his literary
career, no one reading his prose today fails to
appreciate the importance of his contribution
to American Literature.

It is worth noting that practically all the
critical estimates of his work turned in by the
workers on this project, however diversely stated,
recognized Frank Norris' immaturity and grave faults
as a writer, yet realized his significance-- sig-
nificance due to the author's awareness of his
function as a novelist.   Frank Norris, in <u>The
Responsibilities of the Novelist</u>, clearly formulated
his creed:

> "The People have a right to the Truth
> as they have a right to life, liberty
> and the pursuit of happiness.   It is
> <u>not</u> right that they be exploited and
> deceived with false views of life,
> false characters, false sentiment,
> false morality, false history, false
> philosophy, false emotions, false
> heroism, false notions of self-sacri-
> fice, false views of religion, of duty,
> of conduct and of manners."

This creed gave Norris his direction and his
strength.

Most critics are inclined to over-rate the accomplishments of Frank Norris, both as an artist and as a social commentator. His novels are filled with technical defects, and his social philosophy is often shallow, even ludicrous at times. But in spite of these shortcomings, his work, produced in a few years at the turn of the century, is very significant.

Born in a period when the conflicts of social forces were assuming ever greater importance on the American scene, Norris was profoundly influenced by the economic struggle of the time. His awareness of social forces and his theory of literature combined to lead him into a pioneering movement in writing. "The fact is indisputable," he formulated, "that no art that is not in the end understood by the People can live or ever did live a single generation." He went even further to assert that fiction is effective when it "proves something, draws conclusions from a whole congeries of forces."

In _The Octopus_ we find best examplified Norris' theory of the Novel. With telescopic vision Norris sees (though imperfectly) the great "congeries of forces" at work shaping the destiny of man. There is sufficient evidence that Norris failed to understand the implications of these forces at play and the causes of social conflict - but his failure was due to his confusion and his immaturity.

Whatever his limitations as social thinker, he was willing to grapple with broad themes, and to do spadework in cultivating a new growth in literature. It is on the basis of his sincerity and daring that he must be judged; and on the basis of his achievements he will remain one of the most significant of American novelists.

* * * * *

(2)

Frank Norris was one of the first of our realists. He will be long remembered for his contributions to American realism, particularly in McTeague, where, out of intimate knowledge of his subject, he feelingly portrays the life of people caught in the web of life, and makes us, his readers, experience their problems.

Frank Norris was acutely aware that frontiers were no more, that the nation lay in the grip of a struggle to be ceaselessly waged; that the physical frontier was before his very eyes supplanted by the unfenced economic frontier. And despite his confusion, and the mysticism which occasionally invaded his work, he presented life as he saw it, presented it realistically and with fervor.

Because he was among the first to blaze a trail to American realism in literature, and because he was able to instill an epic note into his work, Frank Norris, for all his faults, deserves to be classed among the great.

*   *   *   *   *

(3)

In spite of his announced creed that the people have a right to the truth in literature, Frank Norris fell far short of accomplishing this end in the greater part of his writings.

It is a matter of fact that London, who followed closely in Norris' footsteps, managed to do a better job with similar themes. "Sea Wolf" was undoubtedly suggested to London by "Moran of the Lady Letty"; and "A Man's Woman" suggested "The Mutiny of the Elsinore". And in both instances London surpassed Norris. He was a better craftsman and slightly less inhibited than Norris.

It is quite likely that Frank Norris would have completely freed himself from the shackles of romanticism, were he to mature as a creative writer. But he died when his career had just begun.

*   *   *   *   *

(4)

Although Frank Norris came to California in his boyhood and received most of his formal education in California schools, he was influenced, as a literary craftsman, by the French naturalists rather than the

American realists of his time.   California furnished
the background for his great novels, but his method
of approach he learned from Zola and Flaubert rather
than from Harte, Miller and Mark Twain.

*   *   *   *   *

(5)

Contemporary critics are inclined to classify
Frank Norris as the Boy Zola of the Western World.
But Norris was not a Zola: he was more romantic and
less understanding than Zola.   Norris has also been
compared with Jack London.   This is really amazing.
For the two men had really little in common.   And
of the two Norris was by far the sincerer, the more
original, and the sounder creative writer.

*   *   *   *   *

(6)

Most of Frank Norris' work is devoted to the
description of the trend of living in America.   In
other words, the spirit of a people is revealed to
the reader as Frank Norris sees it.   He has shown
us America with an amazing and uncompromising realism.
He had an invincibly active mind which was never e-
lusive, but made quick contact with its object and
pursued it honestly and implacably to the end.

*   *   *   *   *

(7)

Frank Norris was a master at portraying middle
class people in all their hopelessness and quandries.
In McTeague we see a dentist who just lives, hardly
more, who enjoys picnics and his pot of beer once a
week.   We see McTeague and his fight with his wife
who feared poverty and who ruined her life and those
around her in trying to escape from it.   We see how
impossible it is to escape from the vortex that en-
velopes the struggling middle class, and how more and
more are being sucked down and out from their strata
and forced to accept the struggles of the workers, or
to resignedly give up and accept meekly the few crumbs
that come their way.

Norris is a sociological writer, one not afraid of the truth. His books should remain as part of the heritage and contributions of a society full of contradictions and futility. His life was all too short for a man of his intellectual stature. He was cast upon the scene, and then pulled away without contributing the share of which he seemed overwhelmingly capable.

* * * * *

(8)

Frank Norris was one of the early, if not the first, to write the type of a semi-economic novel, and it was his good luck to be living at the beginning of a new era, in which 18th century methods were to give way to a new literature on the Coast. **All** his efforts were directed to this purpose, and his name will be for all time indelibly engraved on American Fiction, together with Bret Harte and others as the crusaders of this new literature.

* * * * *

(9)

San Francisco can claim Frank Norris as its own. In San Francisco he was nurtured; and San Francisco was the scene of many of his short stories and of his first real triumph with the novel "McTeague."

In all his earlier stories, Norris obviously depended upon plot and exciting incidents to hold the attention of his reader. While his characters were etched sharply and vigorously, they were subservient to the story.

With his novel, "McTeague," Norris definitely departed from his former method. It reveals his determination to no longer depend upon plot but to make human nature the dominating factor. His courage is attested by the fact that he selected the most drab circumstances and the most unsympathetic of characters for his thesis.

In the light of his later books, however, it is important to note that Norris' underlying philosophy in "McTeague" is that the characters are all responsible for their fate. All reaped as they had sown; each brought about their own undoing.

In "The Octopus", and to a greater extent in
"The Pit", we find a reversal of this philosophy.
In "The Octopus" is depicted the strange hold which
a railroad held over a whole state. In "The Pit"
he goes still further, showing that even a strong,
relentless character intent upon power and supremacy
may become a victim of forces stronger than himself.

In thus reversing his philosophy from that of
men being masters of their fate to that of them being
victims of circumstances, Norris was only remaining
true to convictions that the novelist has the duty of
depicting the truth as he sees it. He had become
cognizant of the fact that under modern economic con-
ditions man was no longer a **free** agent but subject to
the stresses of a highly organized society. Believing
this, Norris could not do otherwise than chronicle it
in his work.

* * * * *

(10)

Frank Norris' sense of facts and his patience
in presenting the forces which control these facts
are the secrets of his art. Though he supposedly
came under the influence of Zola, his work refuses to
be classified as naturalistic, realistic, or romantic.
He started out with strong leanings toward romanticism,
and he died before he fully freed himself from the
fascination the romantic school of writing held. His
greatest contribution to American Literature is to be
found in his profound psychological insight into
character and events and in his daring to describe
them truthfully.

* * * * *

Bibliography of Criticism

AIKEN, CHAS. SEDGWICK;
Tribute to Frank Norris
(Sunset, January 1903)

ARMES, WM. DALLAM;
Concerning the Work of the
Late Frank Norris
(Sunset, December 1902)

BEER, THOMAS;   IN   The Mauve Decade (1916)

BLANKENSHIP, RUSSELL;   IN   American Literature (1931)

BOYNTON, PERCY, H: IN   A History of American
Literature   (1919)

"   "   IN   The Rediscovery of the
Frontier (1931)

BURGESS, FRANK GELETT;
One More Tribute to Frank
Norris
(Sunset, January 1903)

CAIRNES, WILLIAM, B: IN   A History of American
Literature   (1930)

Criticisms (cont'd)

CALVERTON, V.F: IN   The Liberation of American
                                        Literature (1932)

CHAMBERLAIN, Wm. FOSDICK: IN   The History of Phi Gamma
                                        Delta (1926)

CHISLETT, WILLIAM, Jr: IN   Moderns and Near Moderns
                                        (1928)

CLIFT, DENNISON, H :   The Artist in Frank Norris
                                        (Pacific Monthly, March 1907)
                                        Republished in the San
                                        Francisco Chronicle -
                                        (June, 28, 1914)

COOPER, FRED. TABER: Frank Norris, Realist
                                        (The Bookman, November,1899)

   "   "   "   Frank Norris
                                        (The Bookman, December, 1902)

   "   "   "   IN   Some American Story
                                        Tellers (1911)

DAVENPORT, ELEANOR, M: Frank Norris
                                        (The U.C. Magazine,
                                        November, 1897)

DELL, FLOYD: Chicago in Fiction
                                        (The Bookman, November,1913)

Criticisms (cont'd)

DOBIE, CHAS. CALDWELL:	Frank Norris, Or Up From Culture (The American Mercury, April, 1928)
DREISER, THEODORE:	Introduction to McTeague Collected Writings,(Vol. 8)
" "	The Early Adventures of Sister Carrie (The Colophon, January, 1931)
EAST, HARRY, M:	A Lesson From Frank Norris (Overland Monthly,December 1912)
ELDREDGE, ZOETH	IN History of California (1915 - Vol. 5)
EDGAR, RANDOLPH:	The Revival of Frank Norris (Boston Evening Transcrpit , May, 3rd, 1930)
EVERETT, WALLACE, W:	Frank Norris in His Chapter (Phi Gamma Delta Magazine, April, 1930)
GARLAND, HAMLIN:	IN Companions on the Trail(1931)
" "	The Works of Frank Norris (The Critic, March 1903)

Criticisms (cont'd)

GILDER, JEANNETTE:

Editorial on Frank Norris
Signed "The Lounger"
(Putnam's Magazine, August 1909)

"   "

Editorial on Frank Norris.
Signed "The Lounger"
(The Critic , May 1899)

GRATTAN, C. HARTLEY:

Frank Norris,
(The Bookman, July 1929)

GOODRICH, ARTHUR:

Frank Norris
(Current Literature,
November, 1902)

"   "

Frank Norris, the Man
(Current Literature,
January, 1903)

HANEY, JOHN LOUIS:

IN   The Story of Our Literature
(1923)

HAZARD, LUCY, L:

IN   The Frontier in American
Literature (1927)

HICKS, GRANVILLE:

IN   The Great Tradition (1933)

HOWELLS, WM. DEAN:

Frank Norris
(North American Review,
December, 1902)

Criticisms (cont'd)

HOWELLS, WM. DEAN: Life and Letters (1928)

___

HUGHES, RUPERT: IN Introduction to Moran of the
Lady Letty - Collected writings
(Vol. 3)

___

HUNT, ROCKWELL, D: IN California and Californians
(1926, Vol. 4)

___

IRWIN, WILL: IN Introduction to The Third
Circle. Republished in
Collected Writings, Vol. 4.

___

KELLNER, LEON: IN American Literature
Translated from German by Julia
Franklin (1915)

___

KNIGHT, GRANT, C: IN The Novel in English (1931)

___

LEISY, ERNEST, E: IN American Literature (1929)

___

LEVICK,MILNE, B: Frank Norris
(Overland Monthly, June 1905)

___

LEWIS, OSCAR: Frank Norris-California Locale
(The Hesperian,Winter Issue 1930)

___

Criticisms (Cont'd)

LEWISOHN, LUDWIG:	IN	Expression in America (1932)
MARBLE, ANNIE RUSSELL:	IN	A Study of the Modern Novel: British and American (1928)
MARCOSSON, ISAAC:	IN	Adventures in Interviewing (1909)
MARKHAM, EDWIN:	IN	California, the Wonderland (1914)
MENCKEN, H. L:	IN	Introduction to Vandover and the Brute. (Collected Writings, Vol. 5)
" "	IN	A Book of Prefaces (1917)
MIGHELS, ELLA STERLING CUMMINS	IN	The Story of the Files (1893)
"	IN	Literary California (1918)
MILLARD, F. BAILEY:		Frank Norris (Out West, January 1903)
MORLEY, CHRISTOPHER:	IN	Introduction to A Man's Woman Collected Writings (Vol. 6)

Criticisms (cont'd)

NORRIS, CHARLES, G:		Frank Norris, 1870-1902 Pamphlet published by Doubleday, Page & Co., (1914)
" "	IN	Introduction to Collected Writings (Vol. 10)
" "		Foreward to Frank Norris of the Wave (1931)
NORRIS, KATHLEEN:	IN	Introduction to Blix (Collected Writings, Vol. 3)
O'DELL, BARRY:		Recollecting Frank Norris (The San Franciscan, December, 1930)
OVERTON, GRANT:	IN	Introduction to The Responsi- bilities of the Novelist (Collected Writings, Vol. 7)
" "	IN	An Hour of the American Novel (1929)
PARRINGTON, VERNON, L:	IN	The Beginnings of Critical Realism in America (1930)
PATTEE, FRED. L:	IN	American Literature Since 1870 (1915)

Criticisms (cont'd)

PATTEE, FRED. L: IN   The New American Literature
                                 (1930)

PHILLIPS, MARION, B: IN   Aspects of the Naturalistic
                                 Novel in America
                                 Master's Thesis. Univ. of
                                 Calif. (1922) (Manuscript)

PRESTON, HARRIET WALTERS   The Novels of Mr. Norris
                                 (The Atlantic Monthly,
                                 May, 1903)

RAINSFORD, W.S: Tribute to Frank Norris
                                 (World's Work, April, 1903)

STEPHENS, HENRY, M: Frank Norris
                                 (Univ. of Calif. Chronicle
                                 January 1903)

TODD, FRANK, M: Frank Norris, Student, Author
                                 and Man
                                 (Univ. of Calif. Magazine
                                 November, 1902)

TOMPKINS, JULIET WILBUR: IN   Introduction to The Pit
                                 (Collected Writings, Vol. 9)

UNDERWOOD, JOHN, CURTIS: IN   Literature and Insurgency (1914)

VAN DOREN, CARL: IN   The American Novel (1921)

Criticisms (cont'd)

VAN DOREN, CARL: IN   Cambridge History of American
                             Literature, (1921)

____

   "   "   AND   IN   American and British
                             Literature Since 1890   (1925)
   "   MARK:

____

WALES, ANITA MARIE: The Development of Frank Norris
                             As a Writer of Fiction
                             Master's Thesis, Univ. of Calif.
                             1918. (Manuscript)

____

WALKER, FRANKLIN :   Frank Norris at the University
                             of California
                             (Univ. of Calif. Chronicle,
                               July, 1931)

____

   "   "   Frank Norris- Biography (1932)

____

WRIGHT, HARRY, M: In Memoriam - Frank Norris
                             (Univ. of Calif. Chronicle
                               October, 1902)

____

ANONYMOUS :   The Persisting Influence of
                             Frank Norris
                             (Current Literature,
                              Febuary , 1912)

____

ANONYMOUS: The Death of Mr. Frank Norris
                             (World's Work, December 1902)

I N D E X

INDEX

BOOKS

<u>Short Stories</u>, <u>Essays</u>, <u>Articles</u>, <u>Reviews</u>, <u>Poems</u> <u>and</u> <u>Plays</u>

<u>C. continued</u>:

<u>Opinions of Leander, The continued</u>: